FESTIVALS and CELEBRATIONS

Eid al-Fitr

By Louise Nelson

KidHaven PUBLISHING

Published in 2023 by
KidHaven Publishing, an Imprint of Greenhaven Publishing, LLC
2544 Clinton St., Buffalo, NY 14224

Written by: Louise Nelson
Edited by: William Anthony
Designed by: Amy Li
Image Credits: All images are courtesy of Shutterstock.com. With thanks to Getty Images, Thinkstock Photo and iStockphoto. Recurring images – RODINA OLENA (pattern), TinyDoz (character), svetichstock , Auspicious, girafchik, kotoffei (vectors). Cover – Hanifah Kurniati, Meranna, Muhamad Norairin Ngateni, Nedim Bajramovic, Magnia, Lionger. 4–5 – JOAT, kiraziku2u. 6–7 – agsaz, Mohamed Reedi. 8–9 – Gabdrakipova Dilyara, Stefan Holm. 10–11 – Lukasz Szwaj, ClassicVector, HappyPictures. 12–13 – Fevziie, Gatot Adri. 14–15 – Dwi Prayoga, Odua Images. 16–17 – onyengradar, SMDSS. 18–19 – ZouZou, Mama Belle and the kids. 20–21 – gulf eye, JOAT. 22–23 – Lukasz Szwaj, Enez Selvi, ClassicVector, deviandalie.

Cataloging-in-Publication Data

Names: Nelson, Louise.
Title: Eid al-Fitr / Louise Nelson.
Description: New York : KidHaven Publishing, 2023. | Series: Festivals and celebrations | Includes glossary and index.
Identifiers: ISBN 9781534543850 (pbk.) | ISBN 9781534543867 (library bound) | ISBN 9781534543874 (ebook)
Subjects: LCSH: Eid al-Fitr--Juvenile literature. | Fasts and feasts--Islam--Juvenile literature.
Classification: LCC BP186.45 N45 2023 | DDC297.3'6--dc23

Manufactured in the United States of America

CPSIA compliance information: Batch #CWKH23: For further information contact Greenhaven Publishing LLC at 1-844-317-7404.

Please visit our website, www.greenhavenpublishing.com.
For a free color catalog of all our high-quality books, call toll free 1-844-317-7404 or fax 1-844-317-7405.
Find us on

Contents

Words that look like <u>this</u> can be found in the glossary on page 24.

What Is a Festival?

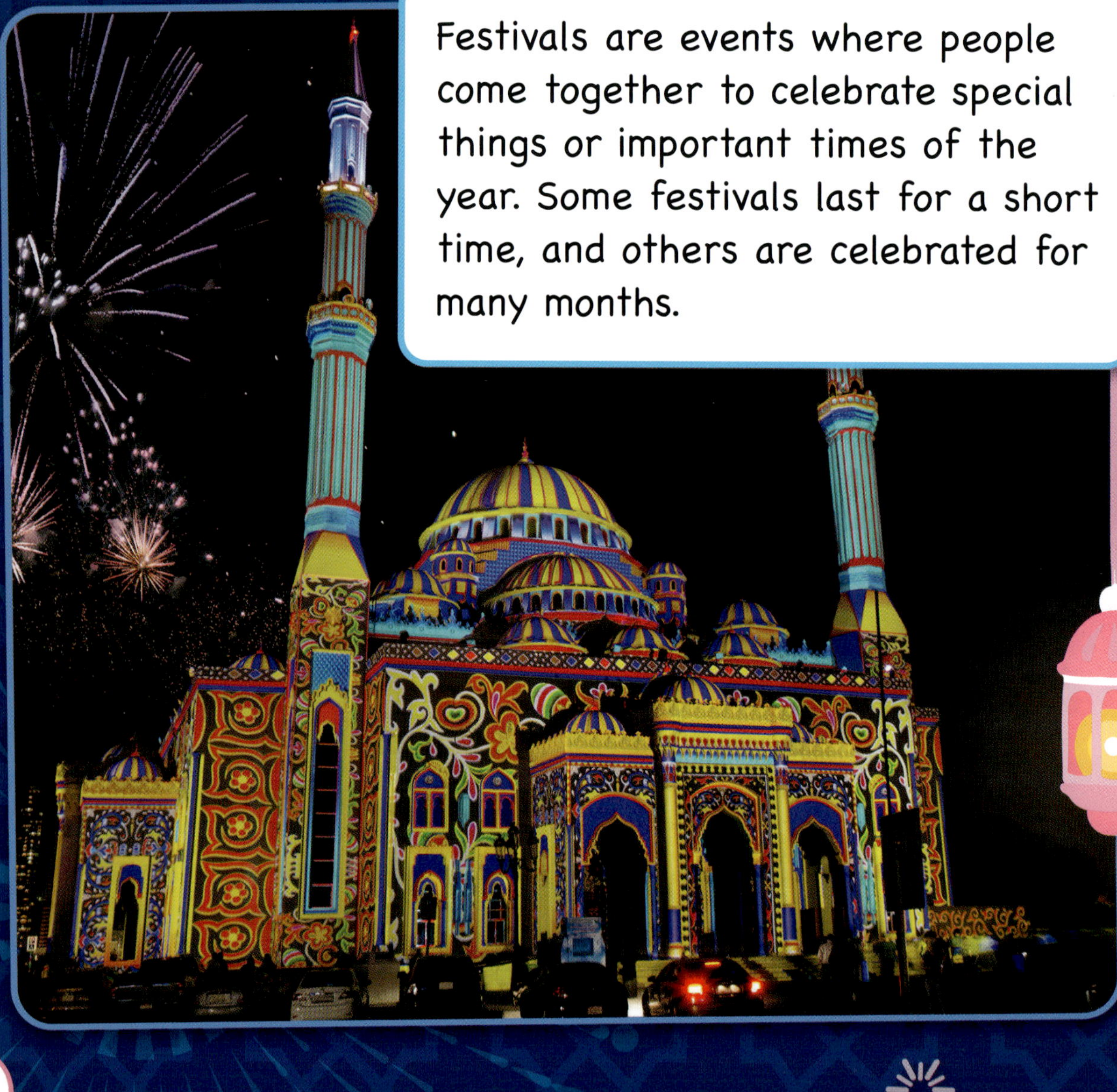

Festivals are events where people come together to celebrate special things or important times of the year. Some festivals last for a short time, and others are celebrated for many months.

There are lots of different festivals. Some festivals are celebrated with a big feast with friends and family. For some festivals, it is traditional to wear certain clothes or dance to music.

Islam

Islam began in Mecca around the year 610 CE. People who follow Islam are called Muslims. Muslims believe there is one God, called Allah. Eid al-Fitr is a festival that is part of Islam.

Islam has a holy book called the Qur'an. Muslims worship in special buildings called mosques. They pray five times a day.

Ramadan and Eid al-Fitr

Eid al-Fitr celebrates the end of Ramadan. Ramadan is the ninth month in the Islamic calendar. Muslims fast while the sun is up during Ramadan to become closer to Allah and understand what it is like to not have enough food.

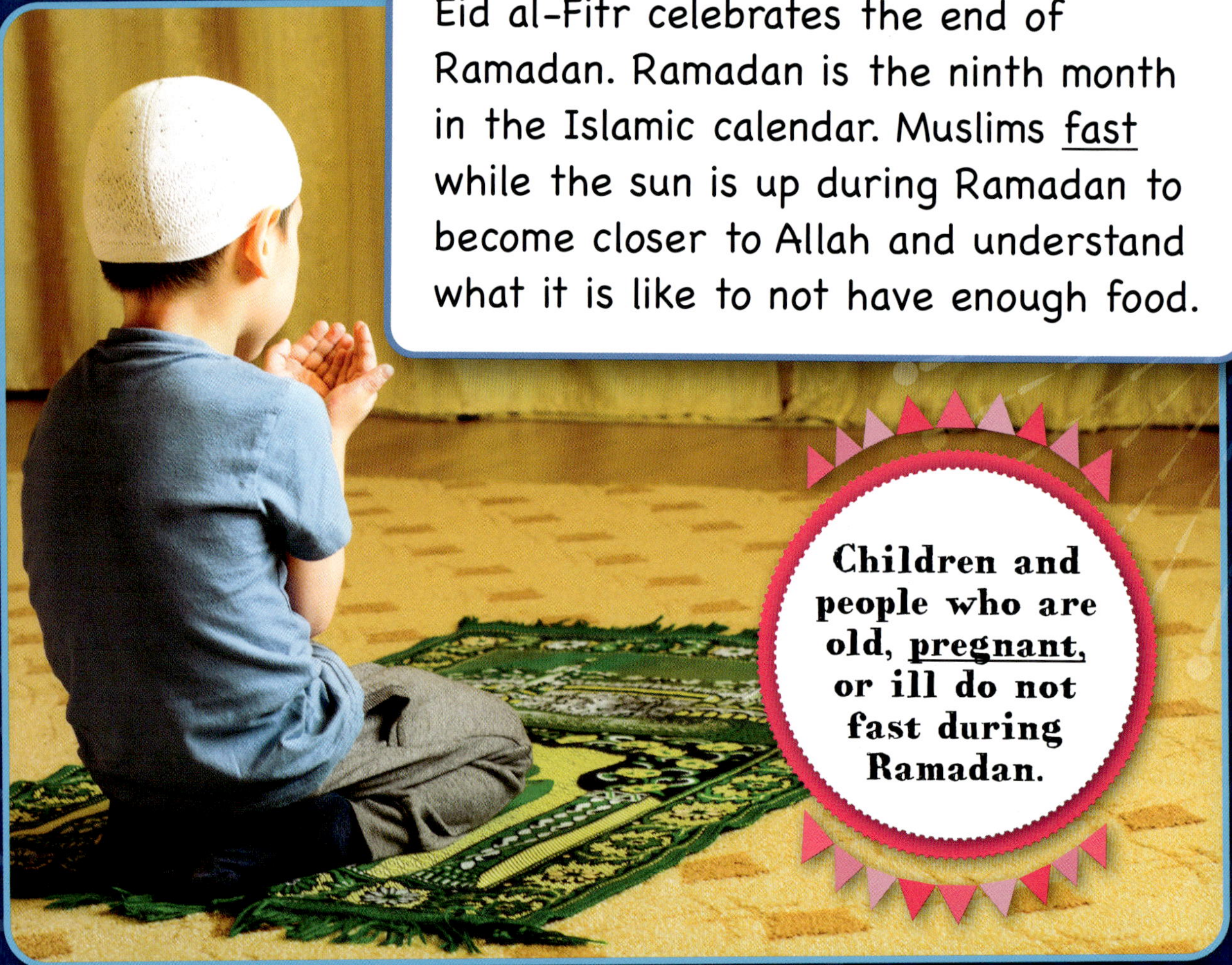

Children and people who are old, pregnant, or ill do not fast during Ramadan.

Muslims celebrate Eid al-Fitr on the first three days of Shawwal. Shawwal is the tenth month of the Islamic calendar. Eid al-Fitr begins when a thin crescent moon is spotted in the sky at the end of Ramadan.

The Story

Muhammad lived in a place called Mecca. In the year 610 CE, he went to a cave in a mountain outside Mecca to meditate.

He heard a voice call out to him. It was the angel Jibreel, the messenger of Allah. Jibreel told Muhammad that he must recite passages that were the words of Allah.

Muhammad began to recite the words of Allah. After this, he made sure the words of Allah were written into a holy book. We now call this holy book the Qur'an.

Muhammad became known as a prophet. Prophet Muhammad traveled far and wide to spread the word of Allah.

This all happened in the month of Ramadan. Muslims remember the meeting of Muhammad and Jibreel and the writing of the Qur'an by fasting during Ramadan.

Helping Others

Before Ramadan ends, grown-ups give money to charity. This is called zakat al-Fitr. It is an important duty for Muslims who can afford to give money. The money goes to helping people who are in need.

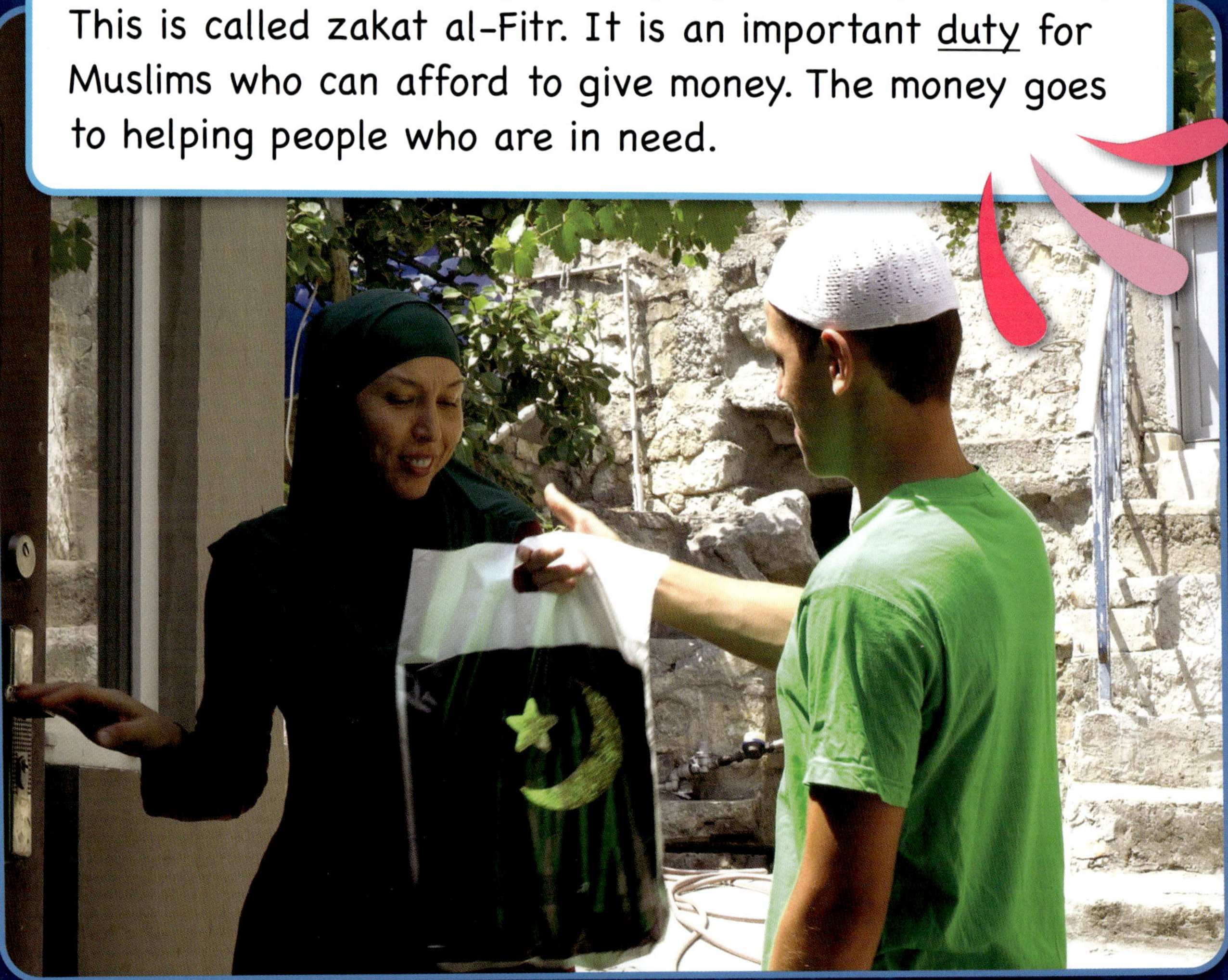

During Ramadan, many Muslims also volunteer to help others. It is important in Islam to help those who are in need.

Salat al-Eid

On the first day of Eid al-Fitr, everybody usually gathers at the mosque for Salat al-Eid. This means Eid prayers. Salat al-Eid happens in the morning, just after sunrise.

There are special prayers for Eid al-Fitr. Muslims worship by reciting the prayers together to feel closer to Allah. After prayers, the imam gives a special talk called a khutbah.

Food

Once Salat al-Eid is over, people gather together to eat. Usually, everybody eats together in the mosque or in the park. There might be a lot of food stalls.

Eid al-Fitr means “Festival of Breaking Fast.”

Many Muslims eat a type of food called sheer khurma. It is made from milk and dates and tastes sweet. It is usually eaten after the prayers in the morning.

Sheer khurma

Clothes

It is traditional for some people to buy new clothes to wear during Eid al-Fitr. They go shopping to buy new clothes for their family.

Many Muslims wear white clothes during Eid al-Fitr. This is because white is a holy color. However, lots of people wear colorful clothes too.

Presents

The celebration of Eid al-Fitr can last up to three days. Many people spend time visiting friends and family. Many people play lots of games and eat food.

Lots of presents are given out between friends and family members. Sometimes, adults give the children money. This is called Eidi.

Eid al-Fitr Around the World

Eid al-Fitr celebrations happen in many different countries because there are many Muslims living all around the world. In Turkey, many people give a food called baklava to each other as presents.

Quiz

What have you learned about Eid al-Fitr?

1. What is the Islamic holy book called?

2. Which month in the Islamic calendar is Ramadan?

3. How many times a day do Muslims typically pray?

4. Where did the Prophet Muhammad live?

5. What time do Eid prayers take place?

Answers: 1. The Qur'an, 2. The ninth month, 3. Five times, 4. Mecca, 5. In the morning, just after sunrise

Glossary

duty something a person must do

fast when somebody does not eat or drink, often for religious reasons

imam somebody who studies Islam and leads prayers at the mosque

meditate to focus the mind, often in silence and usually for religious or relaxation purposes

pregnant when a person has a baby growing inside them

prophet in Islam, someone who is a teacher or carrier of Allah's message

recite to speak words, usually from memory

traditional passed down between people over time

volunteer to work or help without being paid

worship a religious act where a person shows their love for a god

Index